• THE FIRST CUMBRIANS •

H... from Euro... single flint... near Carlis...

Larger g... ...shers and gatherers arrived some 7,000 years ago. Their characteristic small flint tools, known as 'microliths', have been recovered from sites on the Cumbrian coast, such as Drigg, near Ravenglass.

About 6,000 years ago, new waves of immigrants introduced farming into the area. Thus began a long period of clearances of the native forests. These New Stone Age people traded extensively; their goods included products of a stone-axe 'factory' site at Great Langdale in the Lake District. Metal-working, at first with copper and bronze, was introduced about 4,000 years ago. As well as metal tools and weapons, objects from this period include many types of pottery, and jewellery made of gold and jet.

ABOVE: The reconstruction of an Iron Age hut displays important objects from Cumbrian prehistory.

RIGHT: The design of this vessel, which was found near Carlisle, suggests Bronze Age links between Cumbria and Ireland.

BELOW: Bronze Age recycling? An incomplete gold neck-ring, from west Cumbria, which may have been part of a craftsman's stock of this rare metal.

3

THE ROMAN CONQUEST &
· HADRIAN'S WALL ·

At the time of the Roman conquest in AD 43, northern Britain was occupied by the Brigantes, a grouping of smaller tribes which included the Carvetii, who lived in the Carlisle area. They were the descendants of the Celtic iron-using people who had moved into the area around 2,700 years ago. They had brought with them a warrior aristocracy, who lived in defended settlements and employed people to make elaborately decorated metalwork and weapons.

The Roman advance into this area began under the governor Petillius Cerialis, who founded a fort in Carlisle in AD 72, part of which is now covered by the present museum! At first this was a timber building, but it was later rebuilt in stone and continued to be used until the middle of the 4th century.

ABOVE: Discovering Roman remains on the Tullie House fort site (Annetwell Street), 1989.

LEFT: Glass medallion showing the head of the Empress Agrippina – from Stanwix, Carlisle. This was probably a treasured heirloom, worn by an army officer.

Part of Hadrian's Wall near Birdoswald Roman fort. This section of the wall replaced the earlier turf wall, which was on a slightly different alignment.

TVLLIE *house*
MUSEUM & ART GALLERY

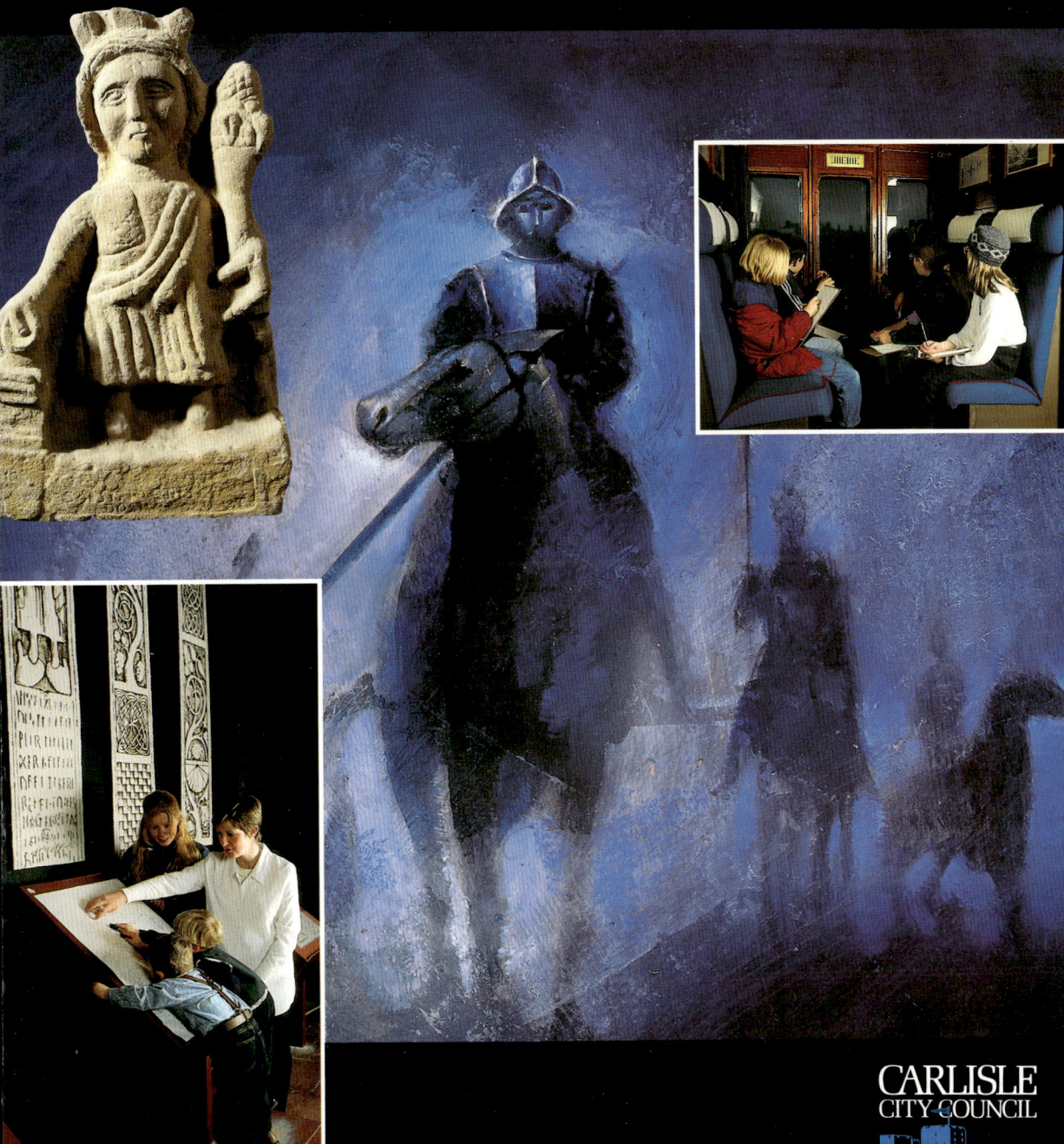

CARLISLE
CITY COUNCIL

FRONT COVER:
RIGHT: Visitors can enjoy both first-class and second-class 'travel' amid the railway displays.
BOTTOM LEFT: Designs from the famous Bewcastle Cross provide a simple interactive feature.
CENTRE: A reiver on horseback; emblem of Tullie House as the Museum of the Border.
TOP LEFT: Roman statuette (genius) from Annetwell Street, Carlisle.

LEFT: Tullie House as it was in 1891 – just before it became a museum – by Thomas Bushby.

RIGHT: The foyer of Tullie House is dominated by the full-size replica of Bewcastle Cross.

BELOW: Discovery drawers in the Wildlife Gallery.

NEW IDEAS ON AN OLD THEME

Tullie House today is a modern museum which owes much to recent developments on both sides of the Atlantic: the accent is on presenting the collections and themes both in a context that interprets the subject matter and in a manner that captivates and enchants the visitor.

Where highly technical methods can aid this interpretation they are brought to bear, but never when a simpler approach is more appropriate. The experience of the visitor is one of discovery, and a great range of subjects is presented in a wealth of different ways.

Alongside the new presentations of existing collections have come developments in storage and computerization which are enabling the museum to cater for the increasing demands for information and access to the rich collections 'behind the scenes'. Emphasis throughout is on access, and on the many and varying needs of visitors and users.

VICTORIAN BEGINNINGS

Carlisle's first public museum opened in 1877 in the Academy of Arts in Finkle Street. It included material from a short-lived museum founded in 1836 by the Carlisle Literary & Philosophical Society.

In the wake of the cultural movement that had started with the Great Exhibition in London in 1851, the citizens of Carlisle had become eager for all kinds of self-improvement. By the 1880s, there was much demand for educational facilities for adults, and for a public library. At the same time the Carlisle School of Art had outgrown its home at the Mechanics Institute and was seeking larger premises to fulfil new ambitions.

MANSION, WAREHOUSE ... AND MUSEUM

Proposals by the architect C. J. Ferguson brought a timely solution. He suggested buying and converting Tullie House, a run-down Jacobean mansion, the stables of which had latterly been used as a cloth warehouse.

His proposals were quickly taken up; he purchased Tullie House and subscriptions were raised from the residents of Carlisle. Some alterations were made to the old house and a completely new range of buildings was added.

Tullie House was handed over to the city and opened in 1893. The new extensions housed a free Library, a School of Art and a Technical School, while the original Tullie House housed the museum, with its collections of Natural History, Archaeology, and Fine and Decorative Arts.

TVLLIE *house*

EXPANSION...

The museum developed as the collections grew. Only when the Technical School and School of Art moved out in the 1950s was any expansion possible. When the Library moved from Tullie House into the Lanes shopping precinct in 1986, far more ambitious plans were laid: there was now a vision of a new museum that would have modern facilities and methods, and act not only as a local and regional focus but also as a national and even an international one.

...AND REDEVELOPMENT

The city's architectural staff provided the design for major extensions; a consultant designer, John Ronayne, led the design of the new displays. The work was completed in 1989/90 at a cost of some £5.25 million. The redeveloped museum was officially opened by Her Majesty The Queen on 3 May 1991 and now receives over a quarter of a million visitors annually.

ABOVE: The new wing of Tullie House (1991), viewed from the castle.

• THE BORDERS BEFORE MAN •

Much of the dramatic countryside of Cumbria and the Borders was shaped during the last Ice Age, which finally came to an end about 13,500 years ago. Ice built up on the high ground and forced its way down the valleys, gouging out the steep sides and flat valley bottoms that we see today. At the height of the last Ice Age the whole region was covered in a great thickness of ice – which reached the highest fell tops. The rocks and debris picked up by the ice were carried many kilometres as the ice flowed slowly across the land.

As the climate warmed and the ice melted, the boulders and clay carried by the ice were deposited on the ground, blanketing the underlying rocks. Plants and animals gradually invaded the ice-free land. At first, the vegetation was tundra-like but, as the climate improved, trees expanded over much of the area, forming vast forests.

This original 'wildwood' was home to large mammals such as red deer, wolves, brown bears and beavers. Eventually, through hunting and loss of their natural habitat, many of the large mammals became extinct in the region. Large predatory birds were also driven out, although the golden eagle, now under protection, still retains a tenuous foothold in the area.

From a cliff near the Wildlife Gallery, a golden eagle overlooks visitors.

RIGHT: Borrowdale as it might have looked during the last Ice Age, by Robert Forrester.

BELOW: After the ice retreated some 13,500 years ago, the purple saxifrage would have been common on the bare, scoured ground; the plant still survives on a few mountain crags.

In AD 122, the Emperor Hadrian visited Britain and ordered the construction of a more permanent frontier across the narrow neck of land from Wallsend (on the east coast) to Bowness-on-Solway. This was to replace the earlier system, based on forts linked by a road, called 'the Stanegate'. The wall is 80 Roman miles (73 modern miles, or 117 kilometres) long and is essentially a system for regulating the frontier. There is a small castle with a gate at each interval of one Roman mile and between each of these 'milecastles' there are two equally spaced turrets.

Other features are a frontal ditch, a road running behind the wall, and a southern boundary ditch – the *vallum* – which probably indicated the extent of the military zone. In addition, several forts were built onto the wall to house the soldiery. It was the building of a second fort, at Stanwix, on the north bank of the River Eden, that had the main effect on Carlisle. This was the largest fort on the wall and housed the cavalry unit, the Ala Petriana.

Because of the presence of the forts, much military equipment has been recovered from Carlisle. This includes awards (the medals of their day), weaponry, identity plates and personal effects. Together these provide an extremely detailed picture of everyday life on the military frontier – a place in which life must often have been extremely hard, basic and unexciting.

LEFT: Openwork sword-belt decoration, showing Jupiter's eagle – from The Swifts, Carlisle.

BELOW: Section of Hadrian's Wall showing the main features of the military zone.

RIGHT: Bronze arm-purse and coins, from Birdoswald Roman fort. This would have belonged to an officer, who must have lost it – along with his savings!

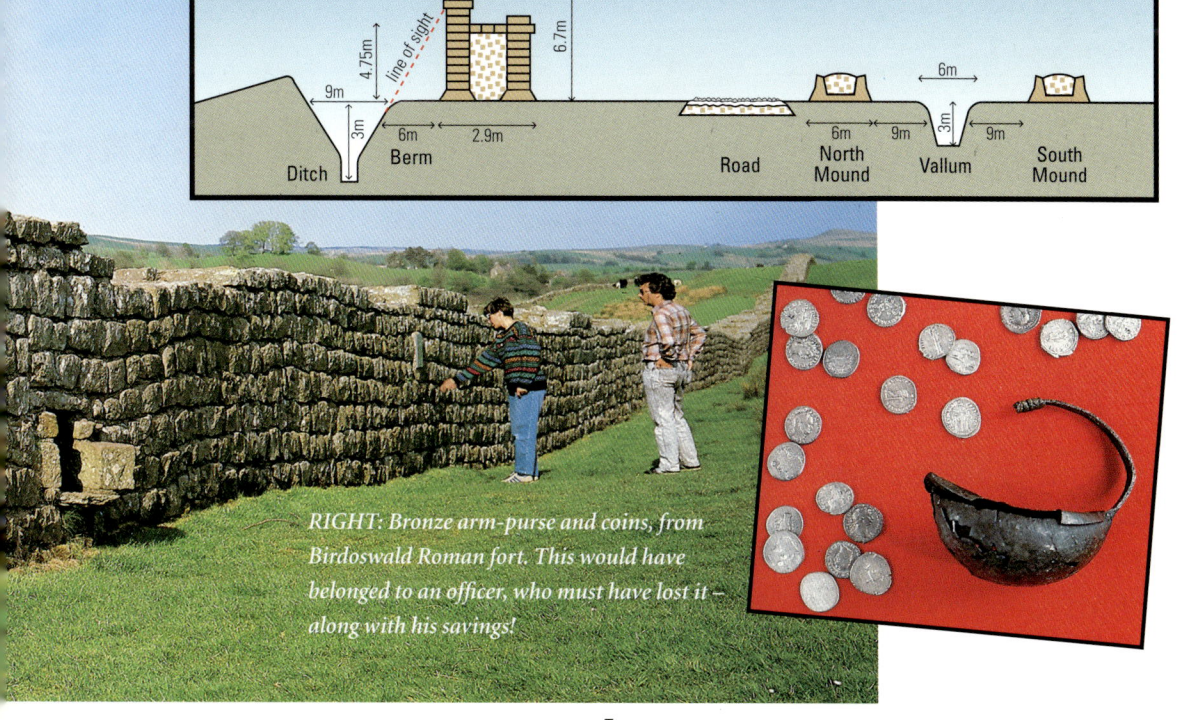

5

• ROMAN CARLISLE •

ABOVE: A funeral procession in the museum's Roman street, with finds from Carlisle.

RIGHT: Statue of the goddess Fortuna from Birdoswald fort on Hadrian's wall.

Roman Carlisle began with the building of the first fort, which now underlies much of the area from Tullie House to Carlisle Castle. The south gateway of the fort proved to be one of the best-preserved examples in Britain. Addresses on locally recovered writing tablets name some of the late-1st-century inhabitants as Domitius Tertius and Marcus Iulius Martialis – the latter living either in Luguvalium (Carlisle) or Trimontium (Newstead, near Melrose, in the Borders). Other evidence shows that people came from distant parts of the empire, such as Flavius Antigonus Papias from Greece, who died in Carlisle.

The presence of the army provided a ready market, stimulating the growth of the town, which eventually became the capital of the tribal area of the Carvetii. The status of the town is shown in its buildings, and by the walled crown on the heads of sculpted *genius* figures, personifying the settlement. Recent excavations have shown that, in addition to a fort, there were houses, some large and built of stone, a possible forum, and at least one bath-house – a hallmark of Roman life.

Archaeologists have shown that the town was part of the mainstream of Roman life in the province. The wealthy were able to import glossy red Samian pottery from France and Germany, as well as mixing bowls and glass from the Rhineland. This last was a Roman introduction and at least some of it was recycled into window panes. That Roman burial practices were also followed is shown by a large tombstone from Murrell Hill, Carlisle. Another tombstone dedication shows that Christianity had just reached the area before the end of the Roman occupation.

The Celtic past of the inhabitants is also demonstrated by the objects which they used. Religion was based on the classical gods such as Jupiter, Mars and Minerva, but local deities such as Cocidius were also worshipped, as can be seen by the silver plaques and altar from the Roman fort site at Bewcastle.

BELOW: Fine tombstones show that important and wealthy people – from distant parts of the empire – lived in Roman Carlisle.

ABOVE: Three finely worked dragonesque brooches showing the swirls characteristic of Celtic art.

• THE DARK AGES •

Following the decline of Roman rule in Britain, Carlisle entered a period dominated by waves of invaders, shadowy British kings and Celtic saints. The area of the city formed part of the kingdom of Rheged, which features in some of the Arthurian romances, and may even have been its capital.

In the 7th century AD, the Angles of Northumbria dominated the region. By this time they had become Christians, and the importance of Carlisle as a religious centre was marked by the visit of Saint Cuthbert in AD 685. The most spectacular of the remains from this chapter of Cumbria's history are the carved stone crosses at Irton (in south-west Cumbria) and Bewcastle (north of Carlisle).

In the second half of the 10th century AD, Viking invaders from Scandinavia began to settle in Cumbria. Although at first they were the looters of legend, they later settled the land and became farmers. In their larger settlements they also became traders and craftspeople.

Analysis of place-names shows the great extent of Viking settlement. It also indicates that the Norwegians came from the west and north – from Ireland, the Isle of Man, Scotland and the Western Isles; by contrast, the Danes came from the south and east, particularly from Yorkshire.

Objects from this period are rare indeed. Those of Anglian origin consist of a few brooches and a disc-headed pin from near Birdoswald. Evidence of a war-like background is seen in the finds from a Viking warrior's burial site at Low Hesket, near Carlisle. Silver ingots from Scotby could also be evidence of looting, but they may have been used in trading. The quality of Viking craft skills can be seen in a silver brooch from Flusco Pike, near Penrith (original in the British Museum).

RIGHT: Bewcastle Cross, one of several finely sculpted Anglian crosses, dating from the 7th/8th century AD. A copy can be seen in the foyer of the museum.

RIGHT: Ritually bent sword from a Viking burial site near Low Hesket, Carlisle. Swords were bent to mark the transition from the earthly world to a spiritual world.

• MEDIEVAL CARLISLE •

In the late 10th century, Malcolm, King of Scots, defeated the Picts and lowland Scotland turned its attention to defending its border with England. Thus began the long and turbulent conflict between the two nations, which was to last until the Union of the Crowns in 1603.

The strategic importance of Carlisle was recognized in 1092, when William II drove the Anglo-Saxon Dolfin from the city. Details of the castle he must have built at this time are difficult to determine because of later additions. The present castle was begun *c.*1122 under Henry I, who also may have provided funds for the city walls.

This strengthening of the defences after the Norman Conquest proved so effective that no Scottish king has since managed to attack the town successfully, despite attempts by William the Lion in the 12th century and Robert the Bruce in the 14th century. Other evidence of this Norman consolidation comes in the records of the names of Norman and Breton lords who were given land-holdings.

Carlisle's importance is also shown by the presence of a Mint, one of only three in the north of England. During the 13th century, silver pennies were minted here, probably in the security of the Castle. Silver for this purpose came from the mines of Alston and Caldbeck.

ABOVE LEFT: Although dating from 1615, this map shows how Carlisle would have looked in the later Middle Ages.

LEFT: Silver pennies of Henry III (1216–72), produced at the Carlisle Mint.

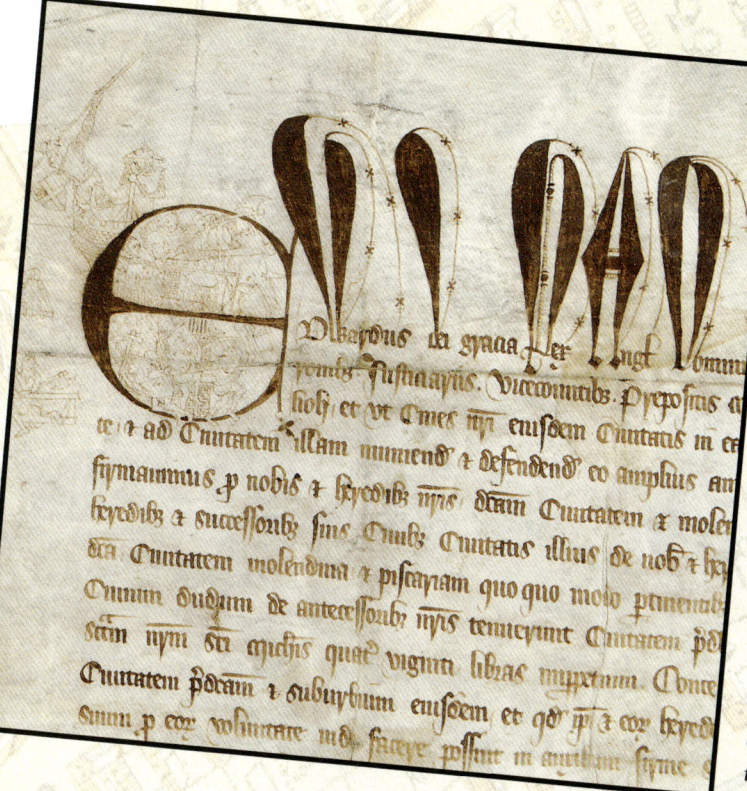

Carlisle was transformed into a city during the Middle Ages by the development of its religious communities. The See of Carlisle had been founded in 1133. The Cathedral Church of St Mary was much extended in the 13th and 14th centuries (although the greatest change was the demolition of most of its Norman nave in 1649). Other religious buildings – now lost – were those of the Blackfriars and the Greyfriars, who had arrived in the 13th century. Two other surviving buildings of the medieval city are the Tithe Barn of St Mary's Priory, and the Guildhall – built as the house of a wealthy merchant and now a small branch museum of Tullie House.

LEFT: *The defence of Carlisle by Andrew de Harcla, illustrated in the initial letter of the 1316 charter granted to the city by Edward II.*

An early safe: iron-bound muniment chest, c.1400 (Guildhall Museum, Carlisle).

• CARLISLE BESIEGED •

In 1641 England was in the grip of Civil War, with the Royalist supporters of King Charles I ranged against Oliver Cromwell's Parliamentarians. The Parliamentarian General Lesley blockaded Carlisle with an army of 4,000 men in October 1644, in the hope of starving its Royalist garrison into submission. The story of the nine-month siege is known from the diary of 18-year-old Isaac Tullie.

Weeks went by and conditions in Carlisle grew steadily worse. By Christmas, all the remaining food in the city was collected together and the citizens and soldiers put on strict rations. Because the city was completely isolated, silver was ordered to be melted down to make coinage – now referred to as 'siege coins'.

In March 1645, King Charles I sent a message saying that he would relieve the city if it could hold out until May. However, this was not to be as he was defeated at the battle of Naseby on 14 June. On 23 June the people of Carlisle could endure the famine no longer. The garrison surrendered and General Lesley granted favourable terms in recognition of their long and brave resistance.

Carlisle was to remain peaceful until 1745. In that year, Prince Charles Edward Stuart ('Bonnie Prince Charlie') travelled from France to Scotland, intending to reclaim the throne for the Stuarts and proclaim his father as King James III.

With his Jacobite followers, he laid siege to the poorly defended Carlisle; the city surrendered on 16 November when the Prince entered the town riding a white charger. Leaving a garrison

BELOW: Prince Charles Edward Stuart, *by Antonio David*.

The South-west Prospect of the Walled City of Carlisle, 1745, by Nathaniel Buck.

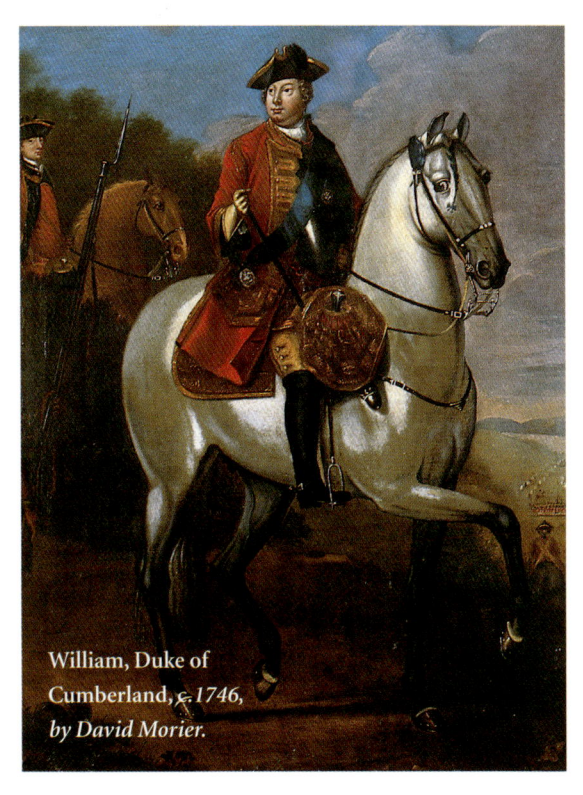

behind, the Highlanders continued south and reached Derby unopposed, but found little support from English Jacobite sympathizers. Reluctantly the Prince turned back – with William, Duke of Cumberland, a son of the King, in hot pursuit.

On 19 December 1745, the Prince re-entered Carlisle briefly before fleeing north. His meagre garrison was unable to defend the city and it surrendered to Cumberland's army on 30 December.

The Duke pursued the Prince northwards and the Jacobites' final infamous and bloody defeat came at Culloden in April 1746. The Prince escaped to France, but his surviving followers were less fortunate. Nearly 400 were captured and brought back to Carlisle; 127 were tried for treason in the Town Hall, 20 of them were hanged on Harraby Hill, and the rest were transported to the colonies or imprisoned.

William, Duke of Cumberland, c.1746, by David Morier.

RIGHT: *During the 1644/5 siege, silver was collected and melted down in order to make coins.*

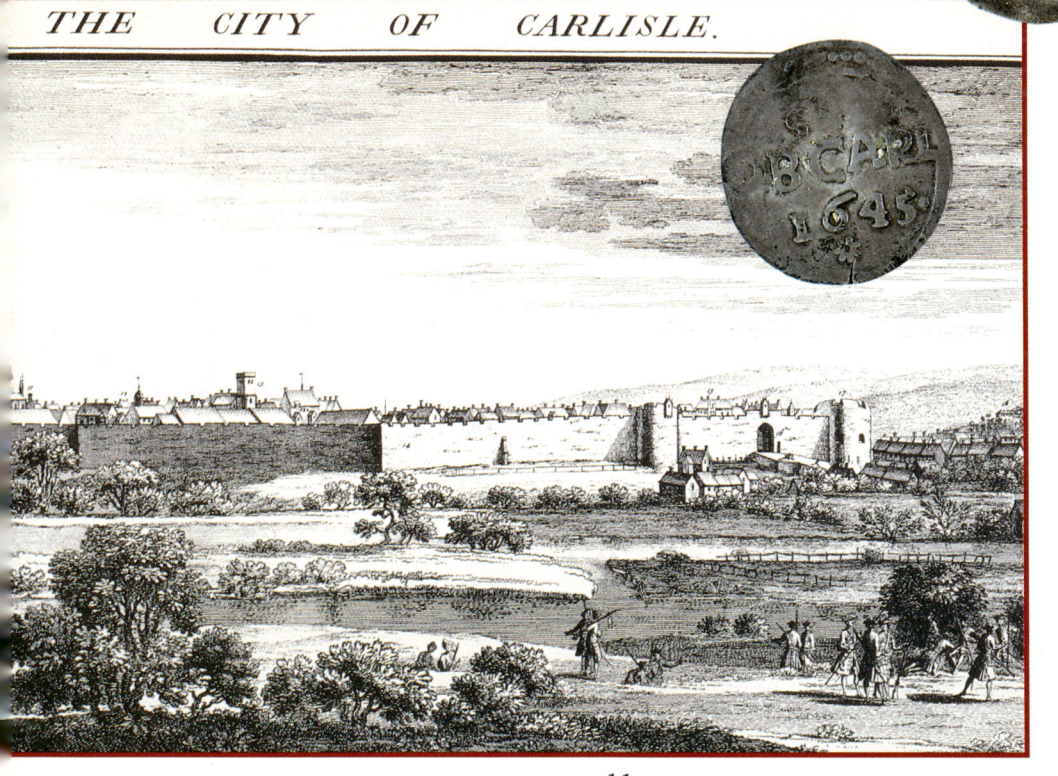

THE CITY OF CARLISLE.

MARKET TOWN TO
• INDUSTRIAL CENTRE •

Carlisle lies on a major trade route at the heart of a large agricultural region. Over the centuries a thriving market town has developed, attracting traders from both sides of the England/Scotland border.

Industrialization began slowly with the opening, in 1747, of a small factory weaving flax into linen. This venture failed but others followed and, within 20 years, cotton cloth called 'calico' was being imported and printed with colourful patterns at the print-works which sprang up beside Carlisle's rivers. Soon calico was being produced locally and the making and finishing of cloth became the city's main industry.

By early 1814, Carlisle was expanding so rapidly that the eastern city walls were demolished to allow more building space.

In the 19th and 20th centuries Carlisle developed a wide range of industries. These included cloth-weaving and printing, biscuit and metal-box manufacture, sweet- and hat-making, and crane and tyre manufacture. The city was also home to building firms which have grown to regional and national importance.

Between 1916 and 1971 Carlisle experienced a nationalization of its pubs and breweries. A 'social experiment' was introduced to see if excessive drinking of alcohol could be controlled by putting the liquor trade under government control. A fascinating episode in Carlisle's history, the scheme introduced many improvements to public-house practice and design.

In 1970 the building of the M6 motorway improved communications with the south and brought new industries to the area. More recently the city has undergone many changes. The pedestrianization of the town centre, the building of the Sands Leisure Centre and the Lanes shopping complex, and the redevelopment of Tullie House have all helped to improve the cultural and leisure facilities in the region.

Cattle Market on the Sands, Carlisle, 1864, by William Henry Nutter.

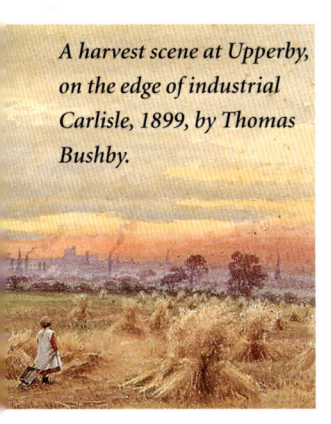

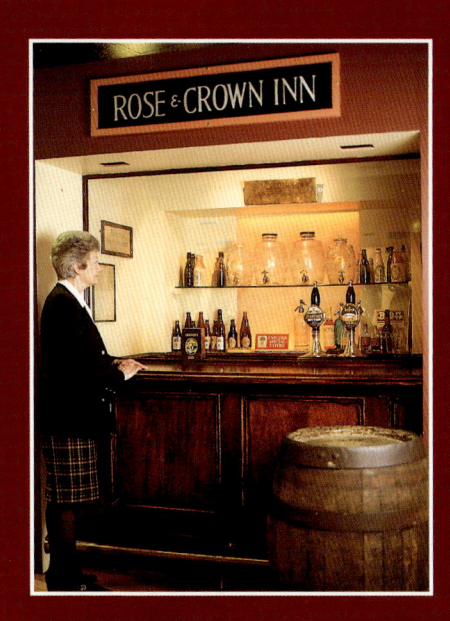

A harvest scene at Upperby, on the edge of industrial Carlisle, 1899, by Thomas Bushby.

LEFT: *The story of the State control of Carlisle's pubs and breweries can be heard in the gallery display.*

BELOW: *Sproat's Cloggers of Rickergate; clogs were the everyday footwear of Carlisle's working people.*

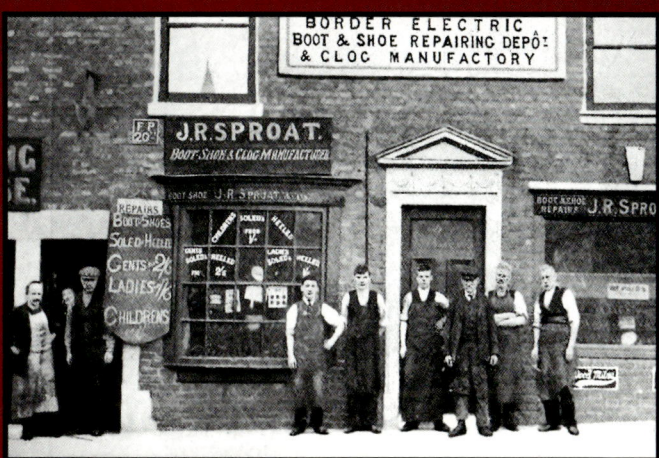

BELOW: *English Street, Carlisle, on a busy market-day in the 1890s.*

13

• THE BORDER REIVERS •

From the 14th to the 17th century, the western end of the border between England and Scotland was a turbulent and lawless place. In these 'Debatable Lands' to the north of Carlisle, the line of the border was not clearly defined. Many lives were lost as local families, like the Armstrongs, Elliots and Grahams, fought to uphold their honour and to expand their property and possessions in this remote land where

LEFT: Hollows Tower on the Border Esk – one of the many fortified buildings which served as strongholds against reiving.

The Reivers: audio-visual presentation.

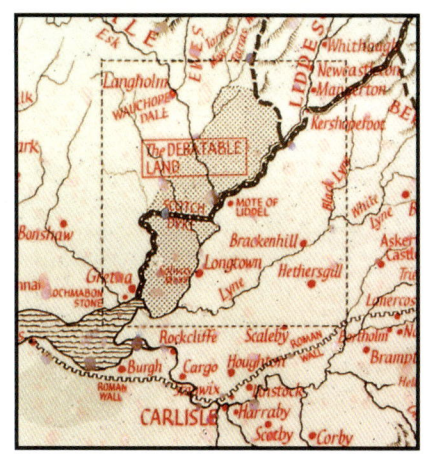

ABOVE: The 'Debatable Land' (shaded).

RIGHT: The reiving families.

no country's laws were respected. These Border 'reivers' (an old name for robbers or bandits) carried out bloodthirsty raids in which victims lost their homes, their cattle and sometimes their lives; what was stolen by one family in a raid was often seized back by their victims at the next opportunity.

Carlisle itself was frequently attacked: fires often swept through the city, destroying the wooden and thatched buildings. Both Henry VIII and Elizabeth I had to order the city and castle walls to be repaired to maintain the defences.

Reiving reached its height in the mid-16th century, by which time many murderous feuds had lasted for generations. In the years following the Union of the Crowns (1603), James I of England/VI of Scotland pursued a determined policy to quell the raiding and impose the rule of national law.

Today, the castles, tower-houses, 'pele' towers and fortified farmhouses dotted around the Border countryside still bear testimony to the harsh rule of 'Border law' in those restless days. The stories of these raids, murders, kidnaps, rustlings and horse-thefts are told in the Border ballads, which began with the reivers themselves and were later collected and promoted by the novelist Sir Walter Scott.

ABOVE: Caldbeck Parish armour, kept to arm volunteers for defence against reiving parties.

> ... There came a man by middle day,
> He spied his sport and went away;
> And brought the king that very night,
> Who broke my bower and slew my knight.
>
> He slew my knight, to me sae dear;
> He slew my knight and poin'd his gear;
> My servants all for life did flee,
> And left me in extremitie.
>
> I sew'd his sheer, making my mane;
> I watch'd the corpse, myself alane;
> I watch'd his body night and day;
> No living creature came that way.
>
> I took his body on my back,
> And whiles I gaed, and whiles I sat;
> I digg'd a grave, and laid him in,
> And happ'd him with the sod sae green...

• CARLISLE: RAILWAY CITY •

Carlisle lies at the crossroads of many routes. It was originally built to defend the western end of Hadrian's Wall, guarding what was to become the England/Scotland border. The city also lies on a major north–south route and, as the road network developed, Carlisle grew into a rich trading town with regular markets.

In the 1790s a plan was put forward to build a canal from Carlisle in the west to Newcastle in the east. This fell through, but in 1823 a smaller canal, linking Carlisle to the Solway Firth, was built. This thrived for a short time but soon became a victim of competition from the railways.

As railways became the principal form of transport, businessmen were quick to realize the importance of Carlisle as a destination. Railway companies were set up on either side of the England/Scotland border, and the city became an important terminus. All goods and passengers had to change trains in Carlisle on their north–south

ABOVE: 1924 poster promoting the London, Midland & Scottish Railway Company.

LEFT: The mock signal gantry symbolizes Carlisle's position at the junction of many routes, both ancient and modern.

RIGHT: Crests of railway companies which used Carlisle before and after the 1923 mergers.

journeys, which created a colourful hustle and bustle at the city's stations. The story of the mergers of the various companies – eventually to become British Rail – is related in the museum displays by a 'Station Announcer'.

At one time as many as seven railway companies had lines terminating in Carlisle, and by 1880 they were all working from the Citadel Station, which had opened in 1847. Over the years, the lives of many of the city's inhabitants have been touched in some fashion by the railways. The significance of this industry to Carlisle, and to its local pride, cannot be underestimated.

The first scheduled mainline electric train (from London to Glasgow) passed through Carlisle on 6 May 1974, marking the demise of steam and heralding a new era of change. The more recent changes are turning rail once more into a privately run network. The major routes still form vital strands in the city's economy, with business links in all directions and the famously scenic Carlisle-to-Settle line appealing especially to visiting tourists.

ABOVE: *Caledonian 78 locomotive beneath the West Walls, Carlisle, in 1869.*

BELOW: *The streamlined* City of Carlisle *locomotive was built in 1939.*

NATURAL HERITAGE
• Moors and Mountains •

The area around Carlisle is renowned for the varied character of its upland landscape, which is a result of differences in rock type. The knobbly granite hills of Galloway on the Scottish side of the Solway contrast with the smooth lines of the Skiddaw Fells of Cumbria, while the hard volcanic rocks of the central Lake District give rise to some spectacular crags. Overlooking the Eden Valley, the steep scarp slope of the Pennines lies along a huge fault in the earth's crust; here thick beds of limestone and sandstones have reared up and now tilt gently down towards the east.

The moors and mountains are home to many specialized plants and animals. The high tops are among the few areas of almost unchanged natural habitat left in Britain but, even here, grazing by sheep has altered the vegetation and wildlife, restricting natural vegetation to inaccessible crags and bogs. The climate at these altitudes is too harsh for many of the common lowland plants and this lack of competition enables some specialist arctic–alpine plants to survive.

Nevertheless, as leisure time becomes more available, human disturbance of these sensitive areas is greatly increasing the amount of pressure on both the landscape and its wildlife.

Peregrine falcon eyrie: peregrines are now widespread in the region, after being almost exterminated by pesticide poisoning.

NATURAL HERITAGE
• Eden Valley •

Woodland diorama: remnants of semi-natural woodland on the steep sides of the River Eden gorge provide a home for a great variety of wildlife; red squirrels are still common here, although they really prefer pine forests.

The River Eden rises in the Pennine Hills and flows north to the Solway Firth. A great variety of plants, insects, fish, mammals and birds live in and along the Eden. The river is one of the cleanest and most species-rich in Britain and, as such, it has been declared a Site of Special Scientific Interest. Fish such as salmon, lamprey and bullhead have important populations on the river and, in recent years, the otter has re-established itself. Threatened species such as the freshwater crayfish and freshwater pearl mussel are also to be found on some stretches of the river.

In the Eden Valley the river flows over red sandstone, which formed as desert sand-dunes some 270 million years ago. In places the river has cut gorges through the sandstone, the steep sides of which still bear some remnants of the natural broad-leaved woodlands that once covered much of the area.

THE DISPLAYS

- The dioramas in the Wildlife Gallery illustrate the habitats and their wildlife along the River Eden, from its source in the Pennines to the Solway.
- On the domed ceiling, bordered by a silhouette of the skyline, a succession of light and sounds – including a passing jet – illustrates the Cumbrian day over an eight-minute cycle.
- The museum's important Natural Science collections – rocks, fossils, minerals, birds, mammals, insects, molluscs and plants – have been built up by naturalists studying and collecting in the area over many years.

The microscopic world of animals and plants is revealed by the gallery microscope.

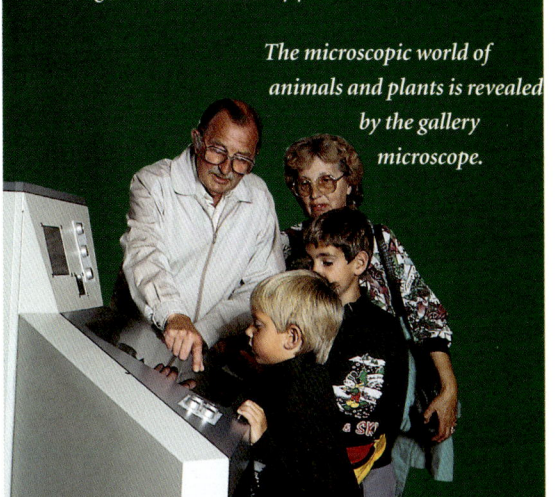

NATURAL HERITAGE
• City Wildlife •

BELOW: *Roof-top diorama: even in the centre of the city, wildlife survives and flourishes – but domestic cats can take a heavy toll of small mammals and birds.*

The rivers flowing through Carlisle act as corridors – bringing the countryside into the heart of the city. Parks and gardens provide havens for wildlife in the built-up areas; derelict industrial sites provide open disturbed ground which can be colonized by many wild plants and animals. The once great railway industry in Carlisle has contracted, leaving many former goods-yards to be reclaimed by nature; several of these are now managed by Carlisle City Council for their wildlife interest.

Even in the most unlikely situations wildlife survives and flourishes. Many plants that escape from gardens grow wild in the city. They are seldom useful as food for native insects, though some, such as buddleia, provide valuable nectar sources for butterflies and hoverflies. The natural balance is disturbed by predators maintained by man – cats and dogs – and much urban wildlife falls victim to these hunters.

Silhouette of the city skyline in the Wildlife Gallery, showing the castle, cathedral and Dixon's chimney.

NATURAL HERITAGE
• The Solway Firth •

Goose diorama: several different kinds of geese visit the Solway each winter. Over the years the once common bean goose has become very rare, while the pink-footed goose has increased in numbers.

Only ten kilometres (about six miles) from Carlisle, the Solway Firth is one of Europe's major estuaries. It is of international importance for wintering flocks of wildfowl and wading birds. Tens of thousands of migrating waders use the estuary as a 'service station' at which to 'refuel' on the plentiful marine invertebrates living in the mudflats before continuing their journeys.

Birds of many species spend the whole winter on the Solway, and the great marshes on the edge of the estuary have long been famous for their wild geese. Some 19,000 barnacle geese from Arctic Spitzbergen return to the Solway each September; pink-footed geese from Iceland are also numerous. The inner Solway is the most important place in Britain for scaup: over 3,000 of these ducks winter on the estuary.

Since early times local people have exploited this natural resource, hunting wildfowl and fishing for salmon and sea trout on the Solway. The traditional hunting methods have now much declined, though they are still practised.

Huge flocks of wading birds visit the Solway as a feeding station on their long migrations.

• TULLIE HOUSE AND THE ARTS •

Tullie House has important collections of Fine and Decorative Arts. Selected aspects of these are featured in Old Tullie House and also appear regularly in temporary exhibitions here, as well as appearing in publications and exhibitions elsewhere in Britain and abroad.

Carlisle became a significant artistic centre in 1823, with the opening of an 'Artists' Academy'. Matthew Ellis Nutter (1795–1862), a Carlisle artist, taught a number of talented pupils at the Academy, including William James Blacklock (1816–58). Nutter's son, William Henry (1819–72), also became a talented artist. Sam Bough RSA (1822–78), perhaps Carlisle's most famous artist, moved to Glasgow in 1848 and finally settled in Edinburgh, becoming one of the leading Victorian landscape-painters in Scotland. Hudson Scott's metal-box factory (now CarnaudMetalbox) brought a number of artists to Carlisle to work in its studio, including the popular Thomas Bushby (1861–1918), who documented many scenes of Carlisle.

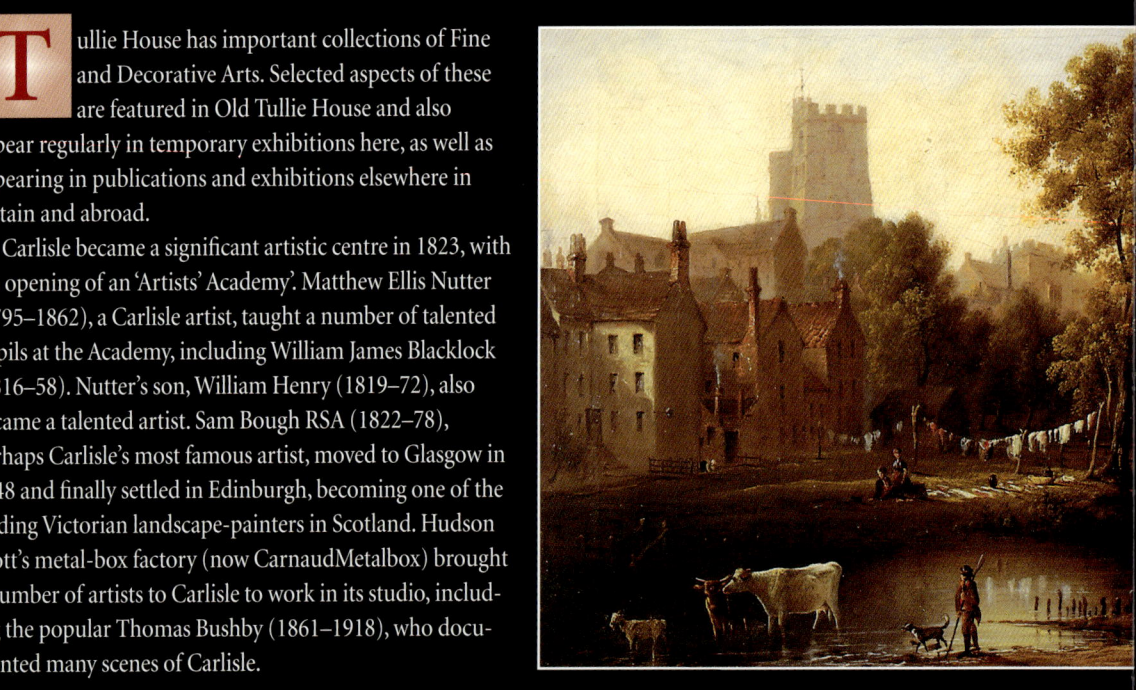

ABOVE: Carlisle Cathedral and Deanery Above Old Caldew Bridge, c.*1815–25*, attributed to Matthew Ellis Nutter: a rare view of the city from the north-west.

LEFT: Baggage Waggons approaching Carlisle, *1849*, by Sam Bough. Baggage waggons followed by weary troops and their families – perhaps returning from Ireland.

BELOW: The Rift in the Lute, *1861/2*, by Arthur Hughes. Inspired by Tennyson's Idylls of the King.

Emily and Gordon Bottomley, of Silverdale, Lancashire, bequeathed their important collection of 600 paintings, drawings and prints to Tullie House in 1949. Bottomley was a poet, playwright and art-collector who had expressed the hope that 'this collection in its entirety might add something permanently valuable to north-country imaginative experience'. Bottomley was impressed by the Pre-Raphaelites and his collection included works by Dante Gabriel Rossetti (1828–82), Sir Edward Coley Burne-Jones (1833–98), Arthur Hughes (1832–1915), Ford Madox Brown (1821–93), William Morris (1834–96) and Elizabeth Siddal (1834–62). He also collected works by his contemporaries, including Paul Nash (1889–1946).

RIGHT: **Easter Monday, c.1954, by Winifred Nicholson (1893–1981), who lived near Carlisle for many years.*

Between 1933 and 1975 the museum operated a scheme for purchasing the work of aspiring young British artists. This scheme relied on the expertise of its honorary advisors – in turn Sir William Rothenstein, Edward Le Bas, Professor Carel Weight and Roger de Grey. This far-sighted initiative enabled the museum to acquire work by artists such as Stanley Spencer, Lucien Pissaro, Wyndham Lewis, Peter Blake and many others.

Robert Hardy Williamson left over 800 pieces of 18th- and 19th-century English porcelain to Tullie House in 1940. Williamson worked in a successful family shipbuilding business in Workington (west Cumbria). His collection of porcelain, which he made at a time when its declining popularity meant affordable prices, is considered one of the best of its kind to have been formed by a private collector. It once adorned Williamson's home at 'Whingarth', Seascale, alongside fine furniture, paintings and clocks. The major English porcelain factories of Chelsea, Derby, Bow and Worcester are well represented, as are the factories of Bristol, Liverpool, Longton Hall, Nantgarw, New Hall, Rockingham, Spode, Staffordshire and Swansea.

BELOW: Derby Campana vase, c.1820, from the Williamson porcelain collection.

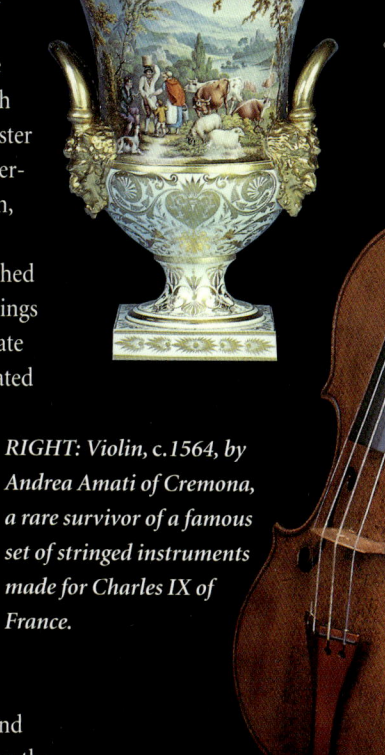

A small collection of musical instruments bequeathed by Miss S. H. Mounsey-Heysham in 1949 includes Strings by three generations of the Forster family, who originate from the area. More important still is the small decorated Amati violin – an international treasure because of its early date and special history.

RIGHT: Violin, c.1564, by Andrea Amati of Cremona, a rare survivor of a famous set of stringed instruments made for Charles IX of France.

The substantial Costume and Textiles collection contains men's, women's and children's costume, and textiles dating from *c.*1750 to the present day. Highlights include a very rare court dress of *c.*1750, wedding dresses dating from 1770 to 1979, men's waistcoats dating from as early as 1765, and some magnificent locally made quilts from the 19th and 20th centuries.

23

• OLD TULLIE HOUSE •

The 1689 frontage of Old Tullie House, facing Abbey Street and the herb garden.

Tullie House today includes buildings of several different periods and architectural styles. The starting point for all this was a large family house associated with the Tullie family. The Tullies were important citizens of Carlisle from at least the early 17th century, as evidenced by Isaac Tullie's diary, which records events of the 1644/5 siege of the city.

When the family first acquired the site it was known as 'The Whitehall'. Thomas Tullie, Dean of Carlisle, rebuilt the property in 1689 as an imposing town house – which we now refer to as 'Old Tullie House'. The building date can be seen on the leadwork of the original rainwater spouts. Its fine Jacobean-style frontage and recent herb garden face onto Abbey Street and the cathedral precinct. Inside the house, a large stone fireplace, oak staircase and the Panelled Room serve as reminders of this period of the building's history.

The house was lived in by the Tullies and their descendants, the Waughs, until 1815. It was sold to the Salkelds, and then the Dixons, and was later leased as a warehouse. By 1890 it had become so dilapidated as to be under threat of demolition.

The Victorian architect C. J. Ferguson raised funds by public appeal to buy the house for the city; outbuildings were demolished and large extensions were added. Notable features from this work include the decorative wall-tiles from the Jackfield tilery in Staffordshire, mosaic floors, and impressive wrought-iron staircases – with heraldic shields based on the city's coat of arms.

Part of the ground floor now forms a Gallery of Childhood and concentrates on the Victorian and Edwardian eras. Themes include the nursery, elementary education, and children at work and play. Dolls, toys and children's costume from the collections can be seen. Important items from the Fine and Decorative Arts collections are exhibited on the staircases and in the Panelled Room on the first floor.

RIGHT: *The Jacobean staircase, c.1689, is one of the surviving features of the original town house.*

BELOW: *Costumed figures in the Victorian foyer of Old Tullie House.*

• BEYOND THE DISPLAYS... •

As an active and developing service, Tullie House performs many functions for its users, who range from visiting tourists to members of the local community, and also include enquirers and researchers from all parts of the world.

COLLECTIONS, INFORMATION AND RESEARCH

Tullie House holds over a quarter of a million objects in the fields of archaeology, history, the arts and natural sciences. A research and enquiry service, based on these important collections and the staff who manage them, is one of the essential functions of Tullie House.

In an age of computerization, data is increasingly being stored and communicated in electronic form. As well as information on the collections, these databases include extensive biological and geological records for the county area.

TEMPORARY EXHIBITIONS

The ultra-modern Art Gallery is one of the largest of its kind in the north of England. It presents touring and home-generated exhibitions in contemporary arts and crafts, and often incorporates material from the museum's own collections. National touring exhibitions have been developed as part of this activity. A programme of temporary exhibitions based directly on the museum's own collections is presented in the Special Exhibitions Gallery, alongside the permanent displays.

EDUCATION SERVICES

Extending Tullie House's interpretive role, its Education staff offer workshops and object-handling sessions, a loans service and teacher training for schools – many of whom are members of our User Group. An educational software programme 'Frontier 2000' (on CD-ROM) has won national awards. Work with the community includes a reminiscence team whose members work voluntarily with the elderly in residential homes in the area.

EVENTS

Events and workshops provided by the City Council's Arts Unit complement the exhibitions and education programmes. The unit operates from Tullie House and also supports a wide range of arts activities and events in the Carlisle area.

FRIENDS OF TULLIE HOUSE

The *Friends* is a local support group and a Registered Charity (No. 1066547). It helps Tullie House with the development of its collections and many other projects.

LEFT: *Collections in store: a vital source for study, research and future exhibitions.*

The Art Gallery provides a major venue for a wide range of high-quality exhibitions of contemporary Arts and Crafts.

LEFT: One of the many volunteers who assist with documenting the collections.

RIGHT: A holiday fancy-dress-making event for all the family.

LEFT: Members of a school class enjoy a workshop session on fossils.

• EXTRA DIMENSIONS •

LEFT: The 98-seat lecture theatre is used for a wide variety of groups, meetings, seminars and conferences.

BELOW: Tullie House restaurant: good food in spacious and elegant surroundings.

The new museum has been designed to cater for the whole community – with accessibility and appeal to families especially in mind. Backed by a friendly and well-informed staff, a full range of support facilities is integral to the operation of Tullie House as a versatile community and visitor attraction. It thus offers a lecture-theatre/function-room suite for conferences, performances and meetings, an activities room, a family restaurant and a well-stocked shop. And there are yet other attractions beyond its walls...

THE GARDEN

The pleasant and secluded grounds of Tullie House provide a haven of tranquillity within the busy Carlisle streets. They were formerly the grounds of the Jacobean mansion, but their original plan is long lost. To complement the house, an attractive herb garden was laid out in 1995 on the Abbey Street side of the building.

The shelter of the buildings gives the grounds an especially mild climate, enabling rare and relatively tender plants to survive. A well-grown specimen of *Catalpa* – the Indian bean tree – dominates the corner next to the University, and fruits in good summers. Strawberry trees (*Arbutus*) also do well here.

At some depth below the surface of the garden lie traces of Roman Carlisle: archaeological excavations carried out in the 1880s and later revealed the foundations of Roman buildings and the line of a Roman road. The road runs towards the south gateway of the fort site which is now partially covered by Tullie House.

RIGHT: The recently established herb garden in front of Tullie House is proving an attractive feature.

LEFT: *The Guildhall, Greenmarket, Carlisle, was once the house of a wealthy merchant. The upper floors of this fine 15th-century half-timbered building form a branch museum of Tullie House.*

THE GUILDHALL MUSEUM

Since 1979 the Guildhall (Greenmarket, Carlisle) has been a small branch museum (Registered No. 161) of Tullie House. One of Carlisle's oldest buildings, it dates from *c.*1405, and much of the original exposed timberwork and internal 'wattle-and-daub' walls still survive. Originally a town house, it became a meeting place for the city's eight Trade Guilds – four of which survive to this day. Items on view include the medieval town chest, as well as Guild objects such as fine silverware and an early banner.

ABOVE: *One of the 'grotesques' from beneath the second-floor projection of the Guildhall Museum.*

In Search of the Border Reivers – The Hot Trod (CD-ROM)

includes hundreds of references to the history of the Border Reivers, their genealogy, poetry, curses and ballads, all set to a background of traditional Border music. Information on a car-trail, accommodation, travel and sales is also given. The many interlinking menus enable swift movement within the program, which features still, audio-visual and video images from many different sources, full-colour imaging and 'morphing'.

AVAILABLE FROM THE TULLIE HOUSE SHOP

Acknowledgements

Photographs on pp. 2 (top left), 3 (top left), 6 (top left and right, bottom right), 14 (main picture), 16 (bottom left), 18–19 (main picture) and back cover were taken by Simon Hill of Scirebröc.
All illustrations are © Tullie House Museum & Art Gallery, except the following:
p. 4 (main picture), Cumbria County Council; p. 10 (top left), Scottish National Portrait Gallery, Edinburgh; p. 21 (bottom), R. Wright.

Text © Tullie House Museum & Art Gallery, Carlisle. Tullie House editor: D. J. Clarke.

Designed by John Buckley.
Edited by Maggie O'Hanlon.

Publication in this form © Pitkin Unichrome Ltd 1998.

No part of this publication may be reproduced by any means without the permission of Pitkin Unichrome Ltd and the copyright holders.

Printed in Great Britain.
ISBN 0 85372 866 6   1/98

BORDER CITY

CITY OF CARLISLE

ALL CHANGE HERE

Tullie House Museum & Art Gallery
Castle Street
Carlisle
CA3 8TP

Tel: 01228 534781
Fax: 01228 810249
E-mail: tullie-house@carlisle-city.gov.uk
Registered Museum No. 160

PITKIN
ISBN 0-85372-866-6

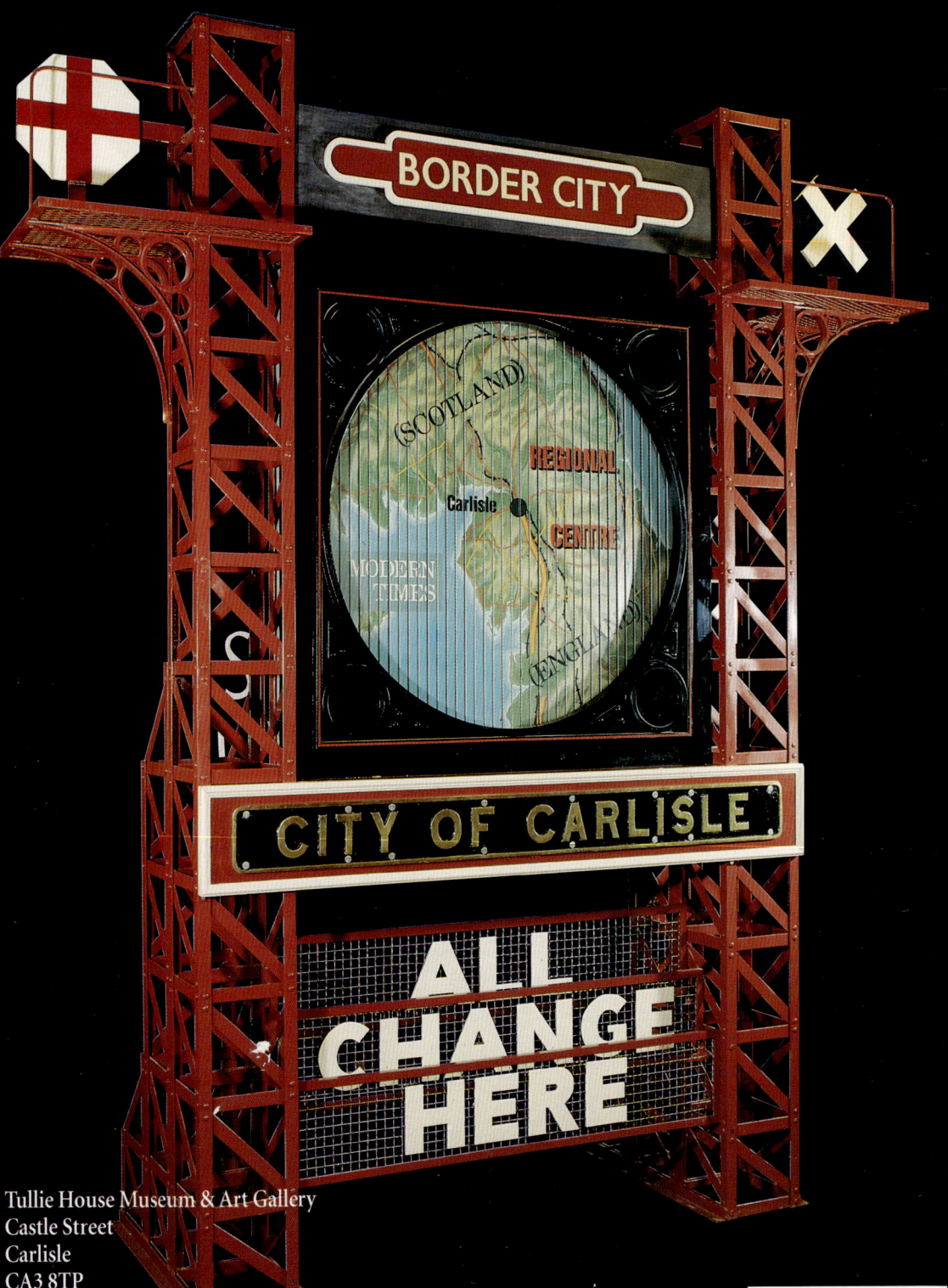

9 780853 728665